Today meets Yesterday
Heute trifft Gestern
Hier/aujourd'hui, mode d'emploi
El hoy se encuentra con el ayer

A book by **Yang Liu**

Transcultural

Transkulturell · **Transculturel** · *Transcultural*

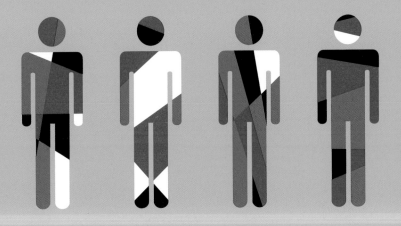

Yang Liu was born in 1976 in Beijing and moved to Germany at the age of 13. After studying at the University of Arts Berlin (UdK), she worked as a designer in Singapore, London, Berlin, and New York. In 2004 she founded her own design studio, which she continues to run today. In addition to holding workshops and lectures at international conferences, she has taught at numerous universities in Germany and abroad. In 2010 she was appointed a professor at the BTK University of Applied Sciences in Berlin. Her works have won numerous prizes in international competitions and can be found in museums and collections all over the world.

Yang Liu lives and works in Berlin.

Photo: Detlef Eden

**EACH AND EVERY TASCHEN BOOK
PLANTS A SEED!**

TASCHEN is a carbon neutral publisher.
Each year, we offset our annual carbon
emissions with carbon credits at the
Instituto Terra, a reforestation program
in Minas Gerais, Brazil, founded by Lélia
and Sebastião Salgado. To find out more
about this ecological partnership, please
check: www.taschen.com/zerocarbon.

**Inspiration: unlimited.
Carbon footprint: zero.**

To stay informed about TASCHEN and our
upcoming titles, please subscribe to
our free magazine at www.taschen.com/
magazine, follow us on Instagram and
Facebook, or e-mail your questions
to contact@taschen.com.

Today meets Yesterday
A book by **Yang Liu**

Idea/Design © Yang Liu

© Copyright of all
artwork and text by
Yang Liu Design
Torstraße 185·10115 Berlin
www.yangliudesign.com

English translation: Hayley Haupt
French translation: Arnaud Briand
Spanish translation: Carme Franch
for Delivering iBooks

© 2022 TASCHEN GmbH
Hohenzollernring 53·50672 Cologne
www.taschen.com

Original edition:
© 2016 TASCHEN GmbH

ISBN 978-3-8365-9214-7

Printed in Slovakia

For Onno & Immi

In 1868, the Chinese emperor sent an envoy by the name of Zhi Gang (志刚) to America and then to Europe to report back on industrialization. Impressed, the scholar told of technological progress and modern production processes, but also of the loss of human values, the pure pursuit of material wealth, and the disappearance of reason. Zhi Gang, like other envoys, feared an excessive use of resources and machines, which replace people more and more and push them out of the focus of creative work. Rather than concentrating on real needs everything was about profit. This way of life went against the traditional Chinese concept of existing in lasting harmony with nature and the heavens.

On the topic of change, opinions have always differed widely. While some delight in progress and the innovations it brings, other mourn after tradition and the good old days. Technological developments obviously bring us many positive advantages, particularly where everyday comforts are concerned. They have come to define lifestyles in big cities all over the world and are now considered status symbols.

Nowadays, we hardly have to move anymore and manage our entire lives with one tiny device. We have come—at least technologically speaking—farther within the past 200 years, than in the millennia before. We have friends around the globe; people from all over the world "like" our posts and can take part in our daily lives. We love transparency and value a hierarchy-free society. An immeasurable amount of information streams through the internet—it seems endless. Our computers are constantly getting faster; human efficiency seems capable of increasing ad infinitum.

What happens in and with us in times like these? How do we handle our changing environment? What exactly are the differences between back then and today? What are the changes doing to our society? How are our habits, perceptions, political stances, values, and, lastly, views of the world changing? Could it be that, along with the many benefits we hope to gain from progress and those that have already manifested, some of the fears held by the Chinese envoy 150 years ago have come true?

I began documenting these changes through my personal experiences and perceptions in pictures. They have been gathered in this book and will hopefully inspire further conversation and exchange.

– Yang Liu

Im Jahr 1868 schickte der chinesische Kaiser einen Gesandten namens Zhi Gang (志刚) nach Amerika und anschließend nach Europa, um von der Industrialisierung zu berichten. Der Gelehrte berichtete begeistert über den technischen Fortschritt und die modernen Herstellungsprozesse, aber auch vom Verlust menschlicher Werte, dem puren Streben nach materiellem Reichtum und dem Verschwinden der Vernunft. Zhi Gang befürchtete, wie auch andere Gesandte, einen übermäßigen Einsatz von Ressourcen und Maschinen, welche die Menschen immer mehr ersetzen und aus dem Zentrum des Schaffens verdrängen würden. Alles konzentriere sich immer mehr auf den Gewinn statt auf die realen Bedürfnisse. Diese Lebensweise laufe der traditionellen chinesischen Vorstellung zuwider, auf lange Zeit im Einklang mit der Natur und dem Himmel zu existieren.

Über Veränderungen gehen seit jeher die Meinungen weit auseinander. Während sich die einen über Fortschritt und die damit verbundenen Erneuerungen freuen, trauern die anderen der Tradition und den guten alten Zeiten nach. Die technologischen Entwicklungen bringen uns sichtlich viele erfreuliche Vorteile, besonders im Bereich des alltäglichen Komforts. Sie bestimmen den Lebensstil aller Metropolen der Welt und sind zum Statussymbol geworden.

Inzwischen müssen wir uns kaum noch bewegen und regeln das ganze Leben durch ein winziges Gerät. Wir sind – zumindest technologisch betrachtet – innerhalb von 200 Jahren weiter gekommen als in den Jahrtausenden davor. Wir haben Freunde rund um den Globus, Menschen aus der gesamten Welt „liken" unsere Beiträge, können an unserem alltäglichen Leben teilhaben. Wir lieben Transparenz und setzen auf eine hierarchiefreie Gesellschaft. Unzählige Informationen strömen durch das Netz, es scheint unerschöpflich. Unsere Computer werden immer schneller, die Effizienz der Menschen scheint unendlich steigerbar zu sein.

Was passiert in und mit uns in so einer Zeit? Wie gehen wir mit unserer sich wandelnden Umgebung um? Was genau sind die Unterschiede zwischen damals und heute? Was machen die Veränderungen mit unserer Gesellschaft? Wie verändern sich unsere Gewohnheiten, Wahrnehmungen, politischen Einstellungen, unsere Werte und letztlich unser Weltbild? Sind vielleicht neben den vielen Vorteilen, die wir uns von der Entwicklung versprechen und die bereits eingetreten sind, doch auch einige der Befürchtungen des chinesischen Gesandten vor 150 Jahren wahr geworden?

Ich habe begonnen, diese Veränderungen anhand meiner persönlichen Erfahrungen und Wahrnehmungen in Bildern festzuhalten. Sie sind hier in diesem Buch zusammengetragen und mögen zu weiterem Gespräch und Austausch anregen.

– Yang Liu

En l'an 1868, l'empereur de Chine confia à l'un de ses émissaires du nom de Zhi Gang (志刚) une mission qui devait le mener d'abord en Amérique, puis en Europe, afin d'y recueillir des informations sur l'industrialisation en cours dans ces contrées. Si le savant brossa un tableau enthousiaste des progrès techniques et des processus de fabrication modernes, il ne manqua pas en revanche d'y évoquer, outre la disparition des valeurs humaines, l'insatiable soif de richesse matérielle et l'égarement de la raison. À l'instar d'autres émissaires, Zhi Gang craignait une exploitation démesurée des ressources et des machines, remplaçant peu à peu les humains et les éloignant de toute activité créatrice. Il observa que tout se concentrait désormais sur le gain et non plus sur les besoins réels de l'homme. Ce mode de vie allait à l'encontre de la vision chinoise tradition-nelle du monde privilégiant l'harmonie durable avec le Ciel et la nature.

Les changements ont toujours nourri des avis opposés. Tandis que les uns se réjouissent du progrès et des innovations qu'il suppose, les autres se bercent dans la nostalgie des traditions et du bon vieux temps. Les avancées technologiques sont synonymes de nombreux avantages, en particulier dans notre confort quotidien. Elles définissent les codes d'un nouveau style urbain aux quatre coins de la planète et s'élèvent au rang de symbole de statut.

Aujourd'hui, nous n'avons quasiment plus besoin de nous déplacer, puisqu'un petit appareil suffit à gérer toute notre vie. Sur l'échelle du temps technologique, nous avons accompli plus de chemin au cours des deux siècles passés qu'au long des millénaires antérieurs. Nous avons des amis sur tous les continents, des inconnus du monde entier « likent » nos publications et peuvent nous suivre dans notre intimité de tous les jours. Nous sommes attachés à la transparence et défendons une société sans hiérarchie. Un nombre infini d'informations circulent sur les réseaux, nos ordinateurs sont de plus en plus rapides, et l'efficacité humaine semble illimitée.

Où cette époque nous conduit-elle et comment nous transforme-t-elle ? Comment appréhendons-nous notre environnement en pleine mutation ? Quelles sont les différences entre hier et aujourd'hui ? En quoi ces changements influencent-ils notre société ? Comment évoluent nos habitudes, nos perceptions, nos convictions politiques, nos valeurs, et aussi notre vision du monde ? À côté des nombreux aspects positifs déjà tangibles ou dont nous espérons bénéficier, certaines des craintes formulées par l'émissaire chinois il y a 150 ans ne se sont-elles pas confirmées ?

J'ai commencé à illustrer ces bouleversements sous forme de pictogrammes en m'inspirant de mon expérience et mes sensations personnelles. Les voici rassemblés dans ce petit livre, en espérant qu'ils donnent lieu à des débats et des échanges fructueux.

– Yang Liu

En 1868, el emperador chino mandó a un emisario llamado Zhi Gang (志刚) de viaje, primero por América y después por Europa, para que recabara información sobre la industrialización. Impresionado, el experto trasladó su visión del progreso tecnológico y los procesos de producción modernos, pero también advirtió de la pérdida de valores humanos, la mera búsqueda de riqueza material y la desaparición de la razón. Como a otros emisarios, a Zhi Gang le preocupaba el abuso de recursos y máquinas, que cada vez más sustituían a las personas y las apartaban del meollo del trabajo creativo. Se dio cuenta de que, en lugar de centrarse en las verdaderas necesidades, lo único que importaba era obtener beneficio. Esta forma de vida iba en contra del concepto tradicional chino que aboga por vivir en larga armonía con la naturaleza y el cielo.

Los cambios siempre han suscitado opiniones encontradas. Mientras que unos celebran el progreso y las innovaciones que este conlleva, otros lamentan la desaparición de la tradición y la gloria de los viejos tiempos. No cabe duda de que los avances tecnológicos ofrecen muchas ventajas, sobre todo en lo que respecta a las comodidades cotidianas. Marcan la pauta del estilo de vida en las grandes ciudades de todo el mundo y se han convertido en símbolo de estatus.

Hoy día apenas tenemos la necesidad de desplazarnos, y gestionamos toda nuestra vida con un minúsculo dispositivo. Al menos en términos tecnológicos, hemos avanzado más en los últimos 200 años que en los milenios precedentes. Tenemos amigos en el mundo entero, desconocidos de todo el planeta que dan al botón «me gusta» de nuestros artículos y pueden formar parte de nuestra vida cotidiana. Nos encanta la transparencia y apostamos por una sociedad sin jerarquías. Por internet circula una cantidad inmensa, por no decir infinita, de información. Nuestros ordenadores son cada vez más rápidos, y la eficiencia humana parece capaz de multiplicarse hasta el infinito.

¿Hasta qué punto influyen estos cambios en nosotros? ¿Cómo manejamos nuestro entorno en constante evolución? ¿Cuáles son las diferencias entre el pasado y el presente? ¿Cómo afectan los cambios a nuestra sociedad? ¿Cómo están evolucionando nuestros hábitos, percepciones, convicciones políticas, valores y, por último, nuestra visión del mundo? ¿Podría ser que, junto a las numerosas ventajas que esperamos obtener del progreso y las que ya se han manifestado, algunos de los temores del emisario chino de hace 150 años se hicieran realidad?

He empezado a documentar estos cambios a través de mis experiencias y percepciones personales y a plasmarlos en ilustraciones. Ahora las he reunido en este libro con la intención de que susciten más debate e inciten al intercambio de opiniones.

– Yang Liu

Breakfast

Frühstück · **Petit-déjeuner** · *Desayuno*

Circle of friends

Freundeskreis · **Cercle d'amis** · *Círculo de amigos*

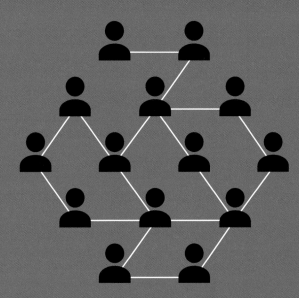

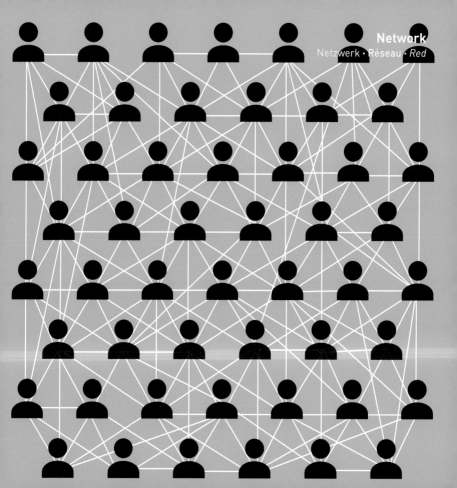

Network
Netzwerk · Réseau · *Red*

Indispensable

Unverzichtbar · **Indispensable** · *Indispensable*

Coffee

Kaffee · **Café** · *Café*

Noise

Geräusche · Environnement sonore
Ruido ambiental

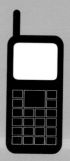

Groups
Gruppierung · **Communauté** · *Grupos*

Concert

Konzert · Concert · *Concierto*

My car

Mein Auto · **Ma voiture** · *Mi coche*

Car sharing
Carsharing · **Covoiturage** · *Coche compartido*

Storage media

Speichermedien · **Supports de stockage** · *Dispositivos de almacenamiento*

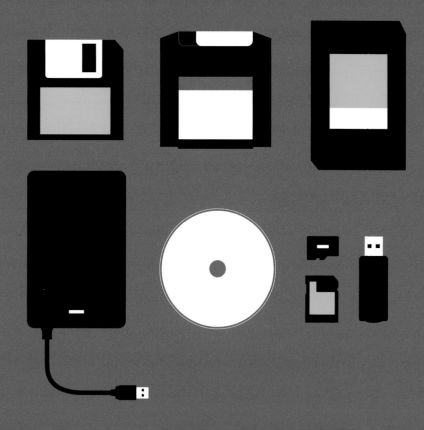

Cloud

Cloud · **Cloud** · *Nube*

Cell phones

Handys · **Téléphones portables** · *Móviles*

Meeting with friends

Freunde treffen · **Réunion d'amis** · *Quedada de amigos*

Metropolises
Metropolen · **Métropoles** · *Metrópolis*

Metropolises

Metropolen · **Métropoles** · *Metrópolis*

1945

need
brauchen · **besoin** · *necesario*

buy
kaufen · **achat** · *comprado*

toss
wegwerfen · **rebut** · *tirado*

need
brauchen · **besoin** · *necesario*

buy
kaufen · **achat** · *comprado*

toss
wegwerfen · **rebut** · *tirado*

Packaging waste

Verpackungsmüll · **Déchets d'emballages** · *Residuos de envases*

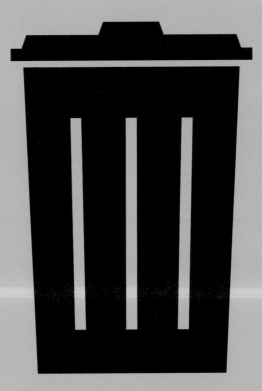

Eating a pizza

Pizza essen · **Soirée pizza** · *Comerse una pizza*

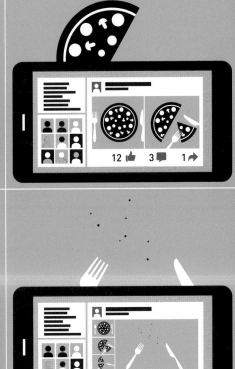

1965

healthy
gesund · **bon pour la santé** · *saludable*

unhealthy
ungesund · **mauvais pour la santé** · *perjudicial*

healthy
gesund · bon pour la santé · *saludable*

unhealthy
ungesund · mauvais pour la santé · *perjudicial*

Demonstration

Demonstration · **Manifestation** · *Manifestación*

Playing
Spielen · **Jouer** · *Jugar*

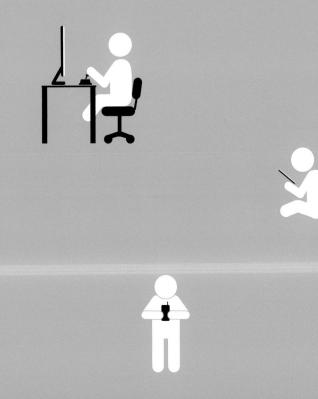

Shortsightedness among children

Kurzsichtigkeit bei Kindern · **Myopie infantile** · *Miopía infantil*

Shortsightedness among children

Kurzsichtigkeit bei Kindern · **Myopie infantile** · *Miopía infantil*

Pedagogics – planning

Pädagogik – Planung · **Pédagogie – apprentissage dirigé** · *Pedagogía – planificación*

Pedagogics – self-determination

Pädagogik – Selbstbestimmung · Pédagogie – autodétermination

Pedagogía – autodeterminación

Refueling
Tanken · **Faire le plein** · *Repostar*

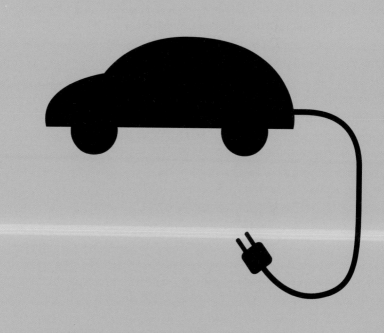

Cucumbers

Gurken · **Concombres** · *Pepinos*

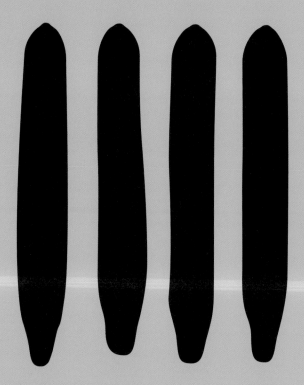

Cucumbers
Gurken · Concombres · *Pepinos*

Nourishing

Nahrhaft · **Bonne chère** · *Nutritivo*

Product testing
Warentest · **Test de produits** · *Prueba de productos*

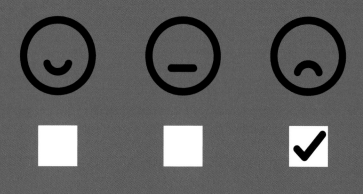

Artisanry

Handwerk · **Artisanat** · *Artesanía*

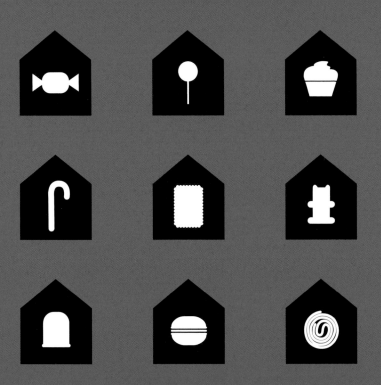

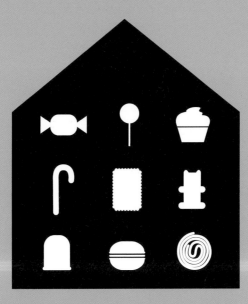

Concentration

Konzentration · **Concentration** · *Concentración*

Phases of concentration

Konzentrationsphasen · **Phases de concentration** · *Fases de concentración*

Individual

Individuum · **Individuel** · *Individual*

Boss
Chef · **Patron** · *Jefe*

Team leader
Teamleiter · Chef d'équipe · *Jefe de equipo*

Formation of worldview
Entstehung des Weltbilds
Apprentissage du monde
Aprendizaje del mundo

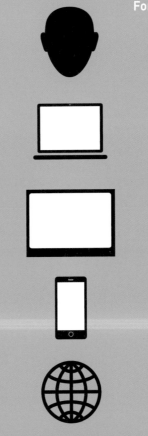

Formation of worldview
Entstehung des Weltbilds
Apprentissage du monde
Aprendizaje del mundo

Leisure – Work
Freizeit – Arbeit · Loisirs – Travail
Ocio – Trabajo

Research

Recherche · **Recherche** · *Investigación*

Research

Recherche · **Recherche** · *Investigación*

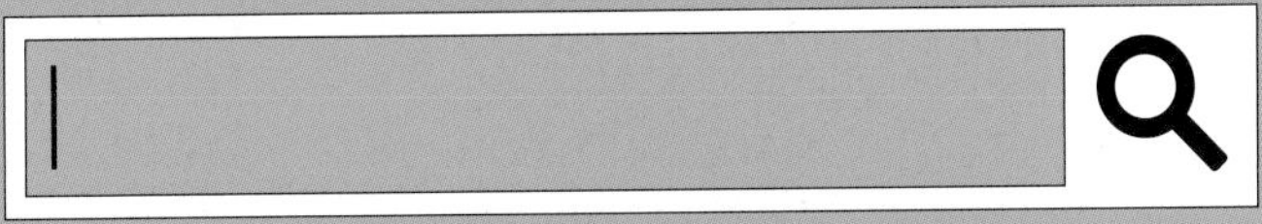

Knowledge

Wissen · **Savoir** · *Conocimiento*

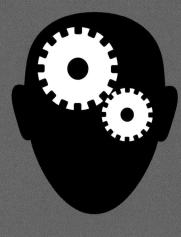

My idea

Meine Idee · **Mon idée** · *Mi idea*

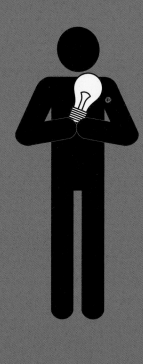

Entrepreneur

Unternehmer · **Chef d'entreprise** · *Empresario*

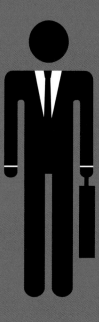

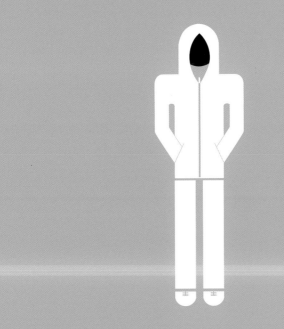

Bank loan

Bankdarlehen · **Prêt bancaire** · *Préstamo*

Countryside – City
Land – Stadt
Campagne – Ville
Campo – Ciudad

Photo

Foto · **Photo** · *Foto*

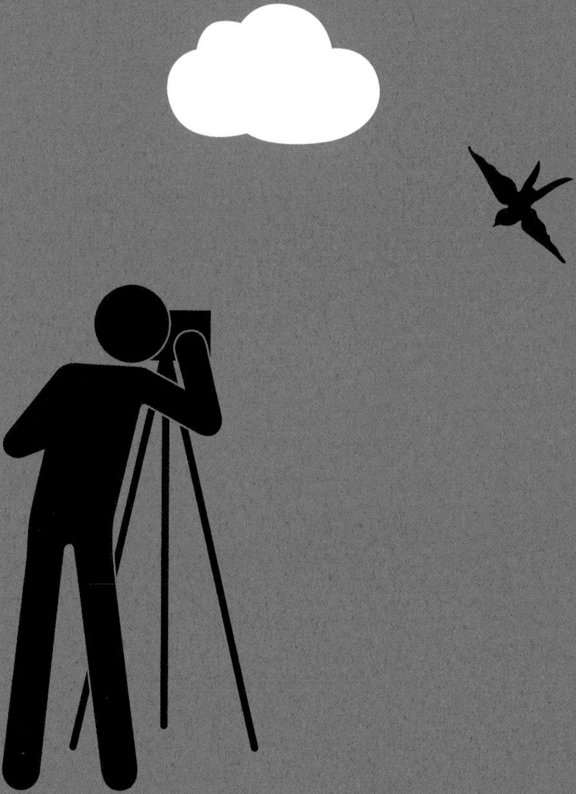

Bullying

Mobbing · **Harcèlement** · *Acoso*

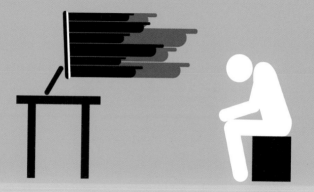

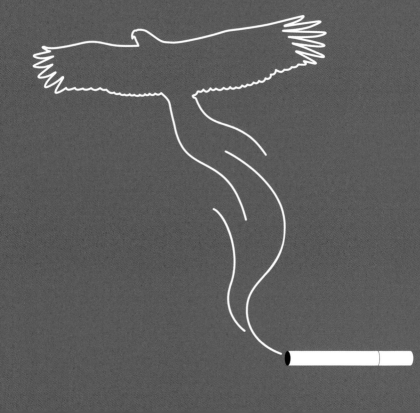

Feeling alive
Lebensgefühl · Se sentir vivant
Sentirse vivo

Risking death
Lebensgefahr · Nuire à la santé
Dañino para la salud

Fur

Pelz · **Fourrure** · *Pieles*

Sheep

Schaf · **Mouton** · *Oveja*

Military intervention

Militäreinsatz · **Intervention militaire** · *Intervención militar*

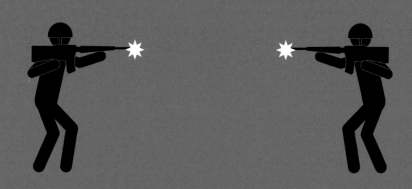

Political goals of major parties
Politische Ziele von großen Parteien
Orientation des principaux partis politiques
Objetivos políticos de los principales partidos

Political goals of major parties
Politische Ziele von großen Parteien
Orientation des principaux partis politiques
Objetivos políticos de los principales partidos

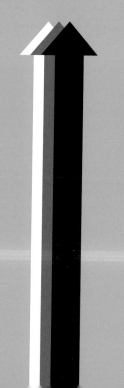

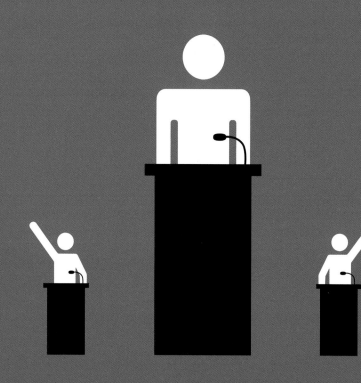

Center ground
Politische Mitte · **Centrisme** · *Centrismo*

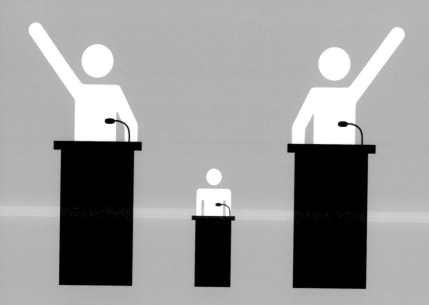

Difference rich – poor

Unterschied Reich – Arm · **Écart riches – pauvres** · *Diferencia ricos – pobres*

Oceans

Ozeane · **Océans** · *Océanos*

Chernobyl 1986

Tschernobyl 1986 · Tchernobyl 1986 · *Chernóbil 1986*

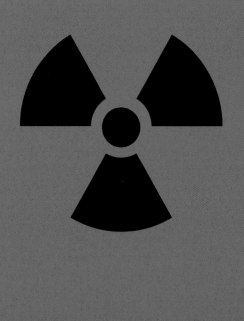

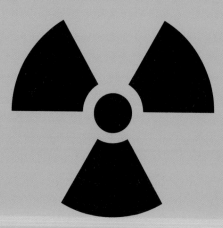

The Arctic

Die Arktis · **L'Arctique** · *El Ártico*

Native peoples

Naturvölker · **Peuples indigènes** · *Pueblos indígenas*

Industrialized Countries – Rest of the World
Industrienationen – Rest der Welt · **Pays Industrialisés – Reste du Monde**
Países Industrializados – Resto del Mundo

Industrialized Countries – Rest of the World
Industrienationen – Rest der Welt · Pays industrialisés – Reste du Monde
Países Industrializados – Resto del Mundo

Western perception of the Middle East

Westliche Wahrnehmung Orient · Le Moyen-Orient vu par l'Occident

Oriente Próximo visto por Occidente

Western perception of the Middle East
Westliche Wahrnehmung Orient · Le Moyen-Orient vu par l'Occident
Oriente Próximo visto por Occidente

Middle Eastern perception of the West

Orientalische Wahrnehmung Abendland · L'Occident vu par le Moyen-Orient

Occidente visto por Oriente Próximo

Middle Eastern perception of the West

Orientalische Wahrnehmung Abendland · L'Occident vu par le Moyen-Orient

Occidente visto por Oriente Próximo

Greek debt crisis
Griechenlandkrise · **Crise de la dette grecque** · *Crisis de la deuda griega*

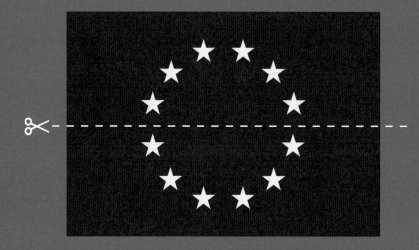

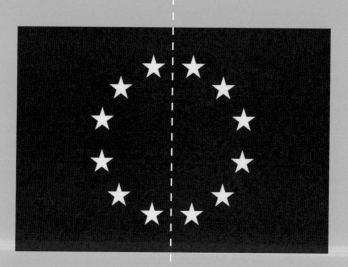

Capitalism – Socialism

Kapitalismus – Sozialismus · **Capitalisme – Socialisme** · *Capitalismo – Socialismo*

Capitalism – Socialism

Kapitalismus – Sozialismus · **Capitalisme – Socialisme** · *Capitalismo – Socialismo*

Power
Macht
Pouvoir
Poder

Power
Macht
Pouvoir
Poder

Children – Adults
Kinder – Erwachsene
Enfants – Adultes
Niños – Adultos

1700

1900

1960

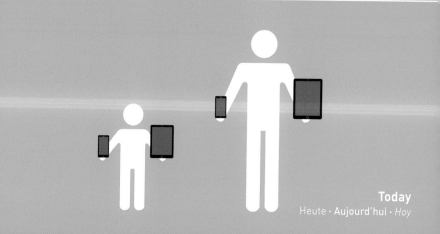

Today
Heute · **Aujourd'hui** · *Hoy*

Economic system
Wirtschaftsform
Modèle économique
Sistema económico

Economic system
Wirtschaftsform
Modèle économique
Sistema económico

Energy
Energie
Énergie
Energía

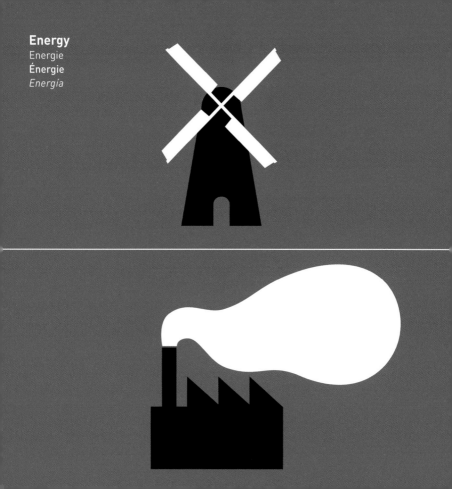

Energy
Energie
Énergie
Energía

Gender equality
Gleichstellung · **Égalité des sexes** · *Igualdad de género*

Industrial Age – Black Lung

Industrielles Zeitalter – Staublunge

Ère Industrielle - Poumons Noirs

Era Industrial – Enfermedad del Minero

Digital Age – Burnout
Digitales Zeitalter – Burnout
Ère Numérique - Burnout
Era Digital – Síndrome del Quemado

Threats
Gefahr
Menaces
Amenazas

1001010111000110011100010
0011111000101101010101100
1001010111000110010010
0010011000101001101110
1010111100011001100010
0111011000011010101110
1010101110000110011000
0101011100000100110001
10010110000011001100010
01101111000000011111100
1010 0010
0 00

Humans – Technology
Mensch – Technik
Homme – Technologie
Humanos – Tecnología

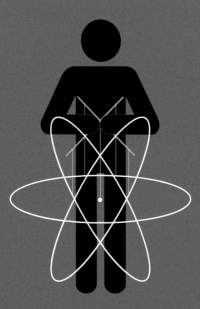

Technology – Humans
Technik – Mensch
Technologie – Homme
Tecnología – Humanos

Neighbors

Nachbarn · **Voisins** · *Vecinos*

Exploitation
Ausbeutung · **Exploitation** · *Explotación*

Danger
Gefahr · **Danger** · *Peligro*

Lifestyle
Lifestyle · Mode de vie
Estilo de vida

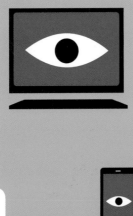

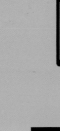

Transparency
Transparenz · **Transparence** · *Transparencia*

Roots

Verwurzelung · **Racines** · *Raíces*

Mobility

Mobilität · **Mobilité** · *Movilidad*

Multicultural

Multikulturell · **Multiculturel** · *Multicultural*